Scandinavian Sweet Treats

Compiled by Karen Berg Douglas

Edited by Miriam Canter, Dorothy Crum, Georgia Heald,
John Zug, and Joan Liffring-Zug Bourret

Cover design by Esther Feske
Cover photograph by Joan Liffring-Zug Bourret shows
Chaston, daughter of Liz (Skaugstad) and John Baker, and
Brett, daughter of Sherry and Chuck Skaugstad, enjoying traditional Chris
at the home of grandparents Marilyn and Dr. Charles Skaugstad, Iowa C

Pen and ink drawings are reproductions of works by Carl Larsson (1853-1919
books and magazines published in Sweden in the collection of John Z. Lofgren.
Carl Larsson is Sweden's beloved artist of family and home scenes.

Special arrangement of Carl Larsson's book plates in Idun magazine, 1913, celebrating his 60th birthday.

ISBN 0-941016-88-9 – Copyright 1992 Penfield Books

Contents

3

Contents *continued*

Contents *continued*

About the Author

Karen Berg Douglas of Lansing, Michigan, is also the author of *Scandinavian Smorgasbord Recipes*, another Penfield Press "stocking stuffer" book in this series. Karen, a daily columnist and feature writer for the *Lansing State Journal*, is of Finnish-Swedish heritage. She co-edited a Scandinavian cookbook for the Scandinavian Society of Greater Lansing. Her recipes have appeared in many cookbooks and periodicals. Many of these recipes come from her personal collection.

Acknowledgments

Our thanks and appreciation to: The Royal Norwegian Embassy; Charlotte J. Anderson, Anderson Butik's Swedish Timber Cottage, Lindsborg, Kansas; Burrell Groups, Ltd.; Norseland Foods, Inc.; Erik Andersen, Andersen Import Service; Marja Lybeck-Pesonen, Vaasa, Finland; Kerstin Olsson Van Gilder, Iowa City, Iowa, and numerous other contributors noted with their recipes.

Scandinavian Sweet Treats

Scandinavians have long held the title of being the greatest coffee drinkers in the world. In fact, visitors to the Nordic countries will find that coffee is served as many as five times a day in some parts of Denmark, Finland, Iceland, Norway, and Sweden.

The true Scandinavian coffee table offers guests more than a simple cup of coffee. Scandinavian hospitality is immeasurable. The host or hostess will go to any length to make guests feel at home. This is generally accomplished through a variety of cookies, cakes, breads, and pastries on the coffee table that will please the palate of the most discriminating guest.

In compiling the recipes for this book I discovered many similarities in the preparation of Scandinavian sweet treats. In recent years there have been a few changes in the types of treats served as well as methods of preparation and storage. However, the concept of the Scandinavian coffee table remains the same. Guests receive a royal welcome, and are treated in the same manner.

—Karen Berg Douglas

Afternoon Coffee in Norway

The table is spread with a beautiful, embroidered white tablecloth for afternoon coffee in Norway. There are always flowers and silver. Tiny demitasse spoons and small cake forks will be on the table if cream layer cake is served. And we always use cloth napkins, or if paper, the same pattern as the dishes if available.

You will find almond cookies, butter cookies, and small tarts filled with almond paste. And you will always find small cardamon doughnuts, *Julekake* (Christmas bread), Napoleons (puff pastry filled with egg cream custard and dusted with confectioner's sugar), and Marzipan Cake filled with apricot jam and whipped cream.

As they say in Norway: *Kakefatene skal bugne!* (The cake platters shall overflow!)
—*Ruth Brunvand, East Lansing, Michigan*

A Danish Coffee Table

During visits with relatives and friends in Denmark, I especially enjoyed the coffee hour. For an afternoon visit, coffee would be served promptly at 2:30 in a smaller room away from the extended tables of the dining room. Following a dinner, it would be served a few hours later and also at a special table away from the meal site.

My first impression of the elegant table is the lovely cloth, usually white, embroidered on linen with deep scallops or lace on the border, falling deeply on all sides of the table. In the center, near the hostess, is the silver coffee service and perhaps a holder for spoons. The china includes demitasse cups to hold the strong black coffee. A small vase or a bowl of garden flowers is a conversation piece.

Varied plates, platters, bowls, and baskets present the pastries, all separate according to kinds and sizes of the cookies and tarts. Silver tongs are used to serve the delicacies which may be eaten with a very small spoon if they are very soft.

continued

One hesitates to compliment the hostess on her baking as she may have shopped for them in several of the bakeries down the street. The conversation is light and in tune with the guests. Their interests, accomplishments, and lifestyles determine what is enjoyable for all. Lingering over each morsel is most enjoyable, since the occasion should be free of commitments that take one away from the table in a hurry!

—Bertha Andersen, Elk Horn, Iowa

Illustration from: Larssons, *1902*

Memories of a Finnish Coffee Table

The Finnish coffee table of my youth, usually a Sunday afternoon with friends dropping by after church, is a sweet and lovely memory. The round table had mother's best white cloth spread upon it.

A special occasion that I recall occurred when father was secretary of a church group. The special *juusto* (oven-baked fresh cheese) had been baked for the occasion. It took 12 quarts of milk, but that was no problem on a farm. Mother also had *piparkakku*—gingersnaps in English. A big sponge cake made with six or eight eggs was also served, as was a special orange cake—a recipe all the ladies used at that time. Of course, no coffee table was respectable if it did not have the beautiful braid of coffee bread, *nisu*, a sweet golden brown loaf flavored with cardamon and sprinkled with sugar. This coffee table was duplicated at Christmas time with the addition of prune tarts, in the shape of stars.

The smell of boiled coffee permeated the big farm kitchen where hand-loomed rugs covered the varnished hardwood floor and the wood stove was polished to a gleam.

—*Eva Ohman Koskimaki, Northville, Michigan*

Remembering Icelandic Sweet Treats

Hot chocolate topped with a spoonful of whipped cream is one of the first things served to a guest in Iceland. This is followed by a wonderful assortment of cookies, crêpes with whipped cream, cakes, tortes, open-faced sandwiches, eggs, herring, and smoked salmon. And everything is topped off with coffee.

I remember one of the last times we visited in 1968 and called on my cousin. She had 27 different things on the table, and she didn't even know we were coming! People in Iceland always treat their guests very specially. They always have coffee in the afternoon and again late at night. One of the things I remember, and which I still do, is serving sugar cubes with the coffee instead of regular sugar.

—Dua Clemensen, Independence, Missouri

A Summer Day Picnic in Sweden

The best way to spend a Swedish summer day is to take a boat ride out to one of the very small islands along the Swedish coast.

In your picnic basket you have coffee and *saft*, open-faced sandwiches, with smoked caviar and sliced hard-boiled eggs; spreadable liver pâté with sliced cucumber, and you will have cinnamon rolls, of course.

However, there is no cinnamon in my favorite rolls. Sprinkle vanilla sugar, along with regular sugar, on the dough instead of cinnamon the next time you bake sweet rolls. It will give a great flavor to your rolls and become a new favorite! And you won't find frosting on your rolls in Sweden. Sprinkle pearl sugar on top of them instead! —*Charlotte J. Anderson, Lindsborg, Kansas*

Coffee, Anyone?

Scandinavians LOVE a cup of richly brewed hot coffee, preferably black! It's usually the first thing they reach for in the morning. It's especially enjoyed in the afternoon with dainty pastries, cookies, and breads. Frequently, coffee is the last beverage consumed before bed in the evening. So, it goes without saying, Scandinavians rarely ask a guest if he or she has time for coffee. The coffee pot is always on!

My parents let me start drinking coffee when I was about four years old, but only on Sunday mornings! It was a treat to look forward to; Mama always made *nisua,* cardamon brown bread, on Saturdays. How well I remember the white porcelain enamel coffee pot boiling on the old gas stove; the rich brown brew perking up into the glass ball at the top. I'd take my place on the red stool in the kitchen and watch as Mama cut a slice of her bread and poured a small cup of coffee for me. There was always a sugar cube or two and a little cream.

Because of time constraints, my husband Phil and I generally brew our coffee electronically these days, but I frequently yearn for the old-fashioned egg coffee that Mama used to make. And, yes, it *does* taste different.

—*Karen Berg Douglas*

Cinnamon Coffee
Finnish

4 cups strong black coffee
1/2 cup cream
1 teaspoon cinnamon
Pinch of nutmeg

4 teaspoons sugar
Whipped cream flavored with a little
   sugar and vanilla

Mix coffee together with the cream, cinnamon, nutmeg, and sugar and keep warm. When ready to serve, pour coffee into cups and top with a spoonful of whipped cream that has been flavored with a little sugar and vanilla. Decorate with a pinch of cinnamon. Serves four.

—*Paulig Coffee Co., Helsinki, Finland*

Finlandia Coffee

1 shot (1 1/2 ozs.) Finlandia vodka
1 shot (1 1/2 ozs.) Arctic cloudberry
liqueur
1 cup hot coffee

1 tablespoon whipped cream
A few Arctic cloudberries

Place ingredients in a glass cup in this order. Serves one.

Fresh Iced Coffee
Finnish

2 cups strong coffee, frozen in cubes
3 cups strong hot coffee

1/4 cup honey
4 teaspoons sugar

Place frozen coffee ice cubes in tall glasses. Filter the strong hot coffee. Sweeten filtered coffee with honey and sugar. Pour the hot sweetened coffee over the cubes. Decorate with a slice of lemon. A drop of rum may be added if desired.

—Paulig Coffee Co., Helsinki, Finland

Illustration from: Ett Hem, *1899*

Old-Fashioned Egg Coffee

8 cups water
6 tablespoons ground coffee

1 egg, slightly beaten
Dash of salt

Heat water in glass or porcelain-enamel coffee pot. Mix coffee grounds with about 1 teaspoon of the slightly beaten egg. (Cover remaining egg and refrigerate for future use.) When water begins to boil, add coffee grounds mixture to boiling water and allow to boil for about 4 to 5 minutes. Remove coffee pot from heat. Sprinkle a few grains of salt into pot, and allow coffee to stand for 3 to 4 minutes, or until grounds settle to the bottom. Serve at once.

—Karen Berg Douglas

Blueberry Muffins

2 cups flour
2 teaspoons baking powder
1 tablespoon sugar
Salt, if desired

1 egg
1 cup milk
3 tablespoons melted butter
  (or corn oil)
1 cup blueberries

Sift together dry ingredients. Beat together egg and milk and add to dry ingredients. Stir in melted butter or oil and blueberries. Divide batter into greased muffin tins. Bake at 400° for 15 to 20 minutes. Makes 12 muffins. Best when made with wild blueberries!

—*Eva Ohman Koskimaki, Northville, Michigan*

Brown Bread
Icelandic

3 packages yeast
1/2 cup warm water
1 cup sugar
3/4 cup molasses
4 1/2 teaspoons salt

3/4 cup shortening, melted
4 1/2 cups water
4 cups whole wheat flour
8 cups white flour

Dissolve yeast in warm water. In a large bowl, combine sugar, molasses, and salt. Mix well. Add shortening and water. Blend in yeast. Add flour, little by little, mixing in well to form dough. Place dough in greased bowl. Heat oven to 350° for 1 minute. Turn oven off. Place bread dough in oven to rise until doubled. Punch down and let rise again. Shape into four loaves and place in greased 9x5x3-inch bread pans to rise again. Bake at 350° for 45 to 60 minutes.

—Evelyn Einarson Holand, Minot, North Dakota

Christmas Bread
Swedish

2 cups lukewarm milk
1 cup sugar
1 teaspoon salt
1 teaspoon ground cardamon
2 packages dry yeast

2 eggs, beaten
4 tablespoons melted butter
7 to 7 1/2 cups flour
1/2 cup citron, chopped fine
1/2 cup raisins

Mix milk, sugar, salt, and cardamon together. Add dry yeast, beaten eggs, and melted butter. Fold in flour and fruit. Knead and place in a well-greased bowl; cover with a damp cloth and let rise until doubled (about 1 1/2 to 2 hours). Punch down and let rise again. Shape into round or braided loaves. Let rise again until double in size. Bake at 350° for 30 to 40 minutes.

Danish Pancakes
Æbleskiver

2 cups flour
1/2 teaspoon salt
1 teaspoon sugar
2 cups buttermilk

2 eggs, separated
1 teaspoon baking soda
Melted butter
Jelly or applesauce

Mix flour, salt, and sugar. Beat together buttermilk and egg yolks; add the flour mixture. Beat egg whites until stiff; add soda, then fold into batter. Heat the æbleskiver pan and put melted butter into each hole in pan. Pour batter into holes, but do not quite fill them. Place over low heat and turn quickly when half-done. Serve hot with jelly or applesauce.
Note: Æbleskiver pans may be purchased at most gourmet cookware shops.

—Hulda Sorensen, Le Claire, Iowa
From: Delectably Danish: Recipes and Traditions

Finnish Coffee Bread

1 cup sugar
1 cup butter (or margarine)
1 teaspoon salt
1 1/2 teaspoons ground cardamon
2 eggs, well-beaten
2 cups scalded milk, cooled
  to lukewarm

2 yeast cakes dissolved in 1/4 cup
  warm water
About 8 cups sifted flour, divided
Melted butter
Glaze:
1 egg
2 tablespoons sugar

In large bowl or pan, mix sugar, butter, salt, and cardamon until fluffy. Add eggs and beat well. Add milk and yeast and stir in about half of the flour. Gradually add remaining flour and knead well until smooth and elastic. Brush top of dough with melted butter. Cover and let rise in a warm place until about double. The dough is ready then to be

continued

Finnish Coffee Bread *continued*

shaped into braids or rolls. Place on greased baking sheets or in pans. Let rise for about an hour. Bake in 350° oven for about 30 minutes.

Glaze:* Beat one egg and 2 tablespoons of sugar and brush top of warm rolls with mixture after taking them out of oven. Cool.

Variation: Add cinnamon to the glaze mixture if this flavor is desired.

—*Pearl Jalkanen, Hancock, Michigan*

Pearl's husband, Reverend Ralph Jalkanen, retired as president of Suomi College in 1990 after 30 years there. Suomi College, located in Hancock, is the only college in the United States founded by Finns.

*If you wish to heed the caution on the consumption of uncooked eggs, we suggest omitting the eggs in the glaze or using a commercial substitute.

Norwegian Cheese Rolls

2 packages dry yeast	4 cups flour
1 1/2 cups warm water, divided	1 teaspoon salt, optional
1/2 cup melted butter	4 eggs, slightly beaten
3 cups Jarlsberg cheese, shredded	1 egg, to brush on top of dough

Soften yeast in 1/2 cup of the water. Combine all ingredients, except one egg, in a large bowl. Mix until you have a soft, smooth dough. With a spoon, make small rolls by dropping about 1 to 2 tablespoons of dough onto a well-greased baking sheet. Let rise until double in size (about 1 to 2 hours). Brush with beaten egg. Bake in a preheated 375° oven for about 15 minutes. Serve warm.

Norwegian Christmas Bread
Julekake

2 packages dry yeast
2 1/2 cups milk, lukewarm
10 to 11 cups all-purpose flour
2 teaspoons ground cardamon
1 1/4 cups sugar

1 1/2 teaspoons salt
1 1/2 cups cold, unsalted butter
2 large eggs, beaten
1 1/2 cups raisins
1 egg yolk
1 tablespoon water

In a small bowl, add yeast to lukewarm milk. In large bowl, combine flour, cardamon, sugar, and salt; mix well. Blend in butter until mixture resembles coarse meal. Add the yeast mixture to the flour mixture. Mix. Add eggs and stir until mixture forms sticky dough. Scrape mixture onto floured board and knead for 8 to 10 minutes until it is smooth and elastic. Knead in raisins. *continued*

Norwegian Christmas Bread *continued*

Form dough into a ball. Place in buttered bowl and turn once to bring buttered side up. Cover bowl with damp cloth. Allow to rise in a warm place for about 1 hour, or until almost doubled. Divide dough into thirds. Form each third into a loaf shape that will fit a buttered loaf pan, about 9x5x3 inches in size. Allow loaves to rise again for about 45 minutes, or until doubled.

Place egg yolk in a cup and add 1 tablespoon water. Beat well, then brush tops of loaves with mixture. Bake in 350° oven for 45 to 50 minutes or until golden brown in color. Turn breads onto metal racks and cool. Makes three loaves.

Illustration from: Larssons, 1902

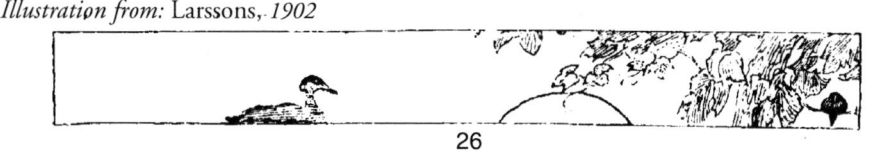

Norwegian Coffee Bread

4 tablespoons butter
4 tablespoons shortening
1 1/2 cups sugar
1/4 teaspoon salt
1 teaspoon crushed cardamon seeds
2 eggs

2 yeast cakes
1 cup lukewarm milk
3 1/2 cups flour
1/2 cup candied fruit peel
Powdered sugar icing

Melt butter and shortening. Stir in sugar, salt, cardamon, and eggs. Dissolve yeast in warm milk. Add flour and the milk mixture alternately to batter. Mix well. Add candied fruit peel. Let rise in warm place until very light (about 2 hours). Knead down on floured board and shape into two 12-inch braids. Place on greased baking sheet and let rise again until light. Bake at 375° for about 20 to 25 minutes. When cool, frost with powdered sugar icing.

Norwegian Date Bread

1 cup dates, chopped
1 cup hot milk
2 cups flour
2 teaspoons baking powder
1 teaspoon salt

1/2 cup sugar
1/2 cup walnuts, chopped
2 cups Jarlsberg cheese, shredded
2 eggs, beaten

Place dates into a large mixing bowl and cover with hot milk. Set aside. In second bowl, combine flour, baking powder, salt, sugar, walnuts, and cheese. Mix well. Stir eggs into date mixture and continue with flour mixture. When well mixed, spoon batter into a well-greased 9x5x3-inch loaf pan. Bake in preheated 325° oven for about 1 hour. Serve hot with butter and jam.

Shrove Tuesday Lenten Buns
Swedish

1 package dry yeast
1/2 cup warm water
1/2 cup half-and-half, lukewarm
1/2 cup melted butter
Filling:
1/2 cup ground blanched almonds
3/4 cup powdered sugar
   (allow additional sugar for sprinkling)

4 tablespoons sugar
3 cups sifted white flour
1 egg, beaten

1 egg white
1 cup cream, whipped

Soften yeast in the 1/2 cup water. Add and mix together half-and-half, melted butter, and sugar. Add flour and mix dough. Allow to rise until about double; then turn onto floured board and knead until smooth and firm. Shape into 12 balls.

29

continued

Lenten Buns *continued*

Arrange, sides touching, on well-buttered baking sheet. Cover with damp cloth and allow to rise again until almost double. Brush with beaten egg and bake at 425° for 15 to 20 minutes, or until brown. Cool.

Filling:
Mix ground almonds, sugar, egg white, and a little water, until smooth. Remove tops from buns. Spread half of each bun with almond filling and add a tablespoon of whipped cream. Replace tops of buns. Sprinkle with powdered sugar. Serve as dessert with hot milk, sugar, and cinnamon.

Note: If you wish to observe the caution on the consumption of uncooked eggs (used here in almond filling), we suggest omitting the egg whites or using a commercial substitute.

Swedish Coffee Bread

1/2 cup shortening
2/3 cup sugar
2 teaspoons salt
1/4 teaspoon crushed cardamon
   seed
2 cups scalded milk
2 packages yeast

1/4 cup lukewarm water
2 beaten eggs
8 cups flour, divided
1 cup white raisins
1 cup citron
1 cup sliced candied cherries
(**Note:** You can use 2 cups diced,
mixed dried, or candied fruit in
place of citron and cherries if
desired.)

Measure shortening, sugar, salt, and crushed cardamon seed into large mixing bowl.
Add scalded milk. Cool to lukewarm and add yeast, softened in lukewarm water. Add
eggs and 4 cups flour. Mix well. Add white raisins, citron, and candied cherries. Beat
in 4 more cups of flour.

continued

Swedish Coffee Bread *continued*

Form dough into a ball and place in greased bowl. Cover and let rise until double. Punch down and knead on lightly floured board. Shape into four braids or four rounded loaves. Place on greased baking sheet and let rise again until almost doubled. Bake at 350° for 30 to 45 minutes. Brush with melted butter or margarine.

Note: Dust warm loaves with a mixture of sugar and cinnamon, or ice with powdered sugar icing for added sweetness and desired taste.

—*Jane Kellon Grein, Bay City, Michigan*

Illustration from: Singoalla, *1894*

Swedish Rusks
Skorpor

1/2 cup butter
1/2 cup margarine
1 3/4 cups sugar
2 eggs
1 teaspoon soda
Pinch of salt

2 teaspoons ground cardamon
3 1/2 cups flour
1 cup sour cream
1 teaspoon lemon juice
1 cup almonds, slivered (optional)

Blend butter and margarine together in large bowl. Add sugar and eggs. Beat well. Sift soda, salt, and ground cardamon with the flour. Add these dry ingredients to butter and egg mixture alternately with sour cream, lemon juice, and almonds. Place dough into two well-greased and floured bread pans. Bake at 350° for 50 to 60 minutes. After removing from oven, cool 10 to 15 minutes before removing from pans.

continued

Swedish Rusks *continued*

Remove bread from pans. When totally cool, slice into 1/2-inch slices. Lay on ungreased cookie sheet. Bake at 350° until brown on each side. Remove from oven. Decrease temperature to 200° and place *Skorpor* in again until hardened and crisp. Store in tins to retain freshness.

Variation: After slicing into 1/2-inch slices, sprinkle with cinnamon and sugar mixture, then place on ungreased cookie sheet to bake at 350° for about 10 to 15 minutes. Remove from oven. Decrease oven temperature to 200° and place *Skorpor* in oven again to get crisp.

Illustration from: Larssons, *1902*

Swedish Saffron Bread

1 package dry yeast
1/4 cup warm water
1/2 cup butter
1 cup light half-and-half cream
1/2 cup sugar
1/2 teaspoon salt

1 egg
1/2 teaspoon powdered saffron
About 4 cups sifted flour
Raisins
1 egg, beaten

In large mixing bowl, dissolve yeast in warm water. In small saucepan, melt butter. Stir in cream and pour the lukewarm mixture into the yeast. Beat in the sugar, salt, egg, and saffron. Gradually stir in the flour and work the dough until smooth. Cover and let rise for 30 minutes. Turn dough onto lightly floured surface and knead until smooth and shiny. Pinch off small pieces of dough; shape into 1/2-inch-wide strips about 7 inches

continued

Swedish Saffron Bread *continued*

long. Shape into fingers, twists, or braids in bun size. Place buns on greased baking sheet and cover with cloth. Let rise until doubled (about 1 hour). Garnish with raisins and brush with beaten egg. Bake in preheated 400° oven for 10 to 12 minutes. Makes about 20 buns.

—*Leo Backman, Stone Mountain, Georgia*

Leo recalls that his mother, Selma Backman, made saffron bread and rolls each December.

Anna Carlson's Meringue Cookies
Swedish

2 egg whites
1 cup sugar
1 tablespoon vinegar

Beat egg whites and sugar together until stiff peaks are formed. Add vinegar. Drop tablespoonsful onto greased cookie sheet. Bake in a 300° oven for 10 to 20 minutes or until dry. Makes about 2 dozen tea-size cookies.

—*Ken Forsman, Dimondale, Michigan*

From: Elias Sehlstedt's Sånger och Visor, *1893*

Chocolate Balls

Finnish

2 cups oatmeal,
   uncooked
1/2 cup melted butter
1 cup sugar

2 tablespoons cocoa
2 tablespoons strong,
   cold coffee
Grated coconut

Combine and mix all ingredients except coconut and roll into small balls. Roll balls in the coconut. Refrigerate for 2 to 3 hours before serving. Store in refrigerator. Makes about 4 dozen.

—*Oy Gustav Paulig AB, Helsinki, Finland*

Cranberry-Apricot Tart

Pastry:
6 tablespoons butter, cut into bits
1/2 cup shredded gjetost cheese
1 cup unsifted flour
2 tablespoons sugar
1 teaspoon grated orange peel
1 egg
1 tablespoon ice water

Filling:
4 cups coarsely chopped cranberries
3/4 cup sugar
1 teaspoon lemon juice
1 16-ounce can apricot halves,
  drained
Sweetened whipped cream

Pastry: In food processor, blend butter and cheese into flour. Add sugar and orange peel. Blend in egg, using on and off switch. Add water. When well-blended, remove dough and press against sides and bottom of a 9-inch tart pan with removable bottom. **Filling:** Combine cranberries, sugar, and lemon juice. Pour into crust. Saving three halves for center garnish, cut remaining apricots in half. Arrange on top of cranberries. Bake at 425° for 20 minutes. Cool in pan. To serve, garnish with whipped cream, if desired. Makes one 9-inch pie.

Danish Crown Cookies

Traesko Klampe

1 cup sugar
1 cup lard
1 cup molasses
1/2 teaspoon salt

1 teaspoon soda
Cinnamon and cloves
Enough flour to make a workable
    dough

Combine sugar, lard, and molasses and cook until mixture boils. Add salt, soda, and spices to taste. Scald mixture. Place in mixing bowl and allow to cool; when cooled, add the flour and mix to form dough. Roll into 12-inch lengths and place in refrigerator. When hard, cut slices and place on cookie sheet. Decorate with a blanched almond on each cookie. Bake at 325° for 10 to 12 minutes, or until done. Makes about 5 dozen cookies.

—*Bertha Andersen, Elk Horn, Iowa*

Danish Crullers
Klejner

3 egg yolks
3 tablespoons sugar
3 tablespoons heavy cream

1/2 teaspoon cardamon
1 to 1 1/2 cups flour
Pinch of salt

Mix all ingredients together to make a soft dough. Roll very thin on a floured board. Cut in strips 1 inch wide with a diagonal cut every 4-inch length. Make a slit in the center. Slip one end through the slit, making a twist. Fry in deep fat at 350° until brown. Makes about 4 dozen.

—*Bertha Andersen, Elk Horn, Iowa*

41

Danish Pastry Strips
Wienerbrød

1 package yeast
1/4 cup warm water
1 cup milk
1 egg
10 cardamon seeds, crushed
1 1/2 tablespoons sugar

1/2 teaspoon salt
3 cups flour
1 cup butter, cut into bits, divided
Melted butter for brushing top
Powdered sugar icing
Sliced almonds

Sprinkle yeast over warm water in small cup and let stand 10 minutes. Then place in a bowl with the milk, egg, cardamon, sugar, and salt. Mix well. Add the flour and work into dough. Place dough on floured board and roll into a square. Place about 1/8 of the butter in the center and fold the sides and ends over the center. Roll out and fold again

continued

Danish Pastry Strips *continued*

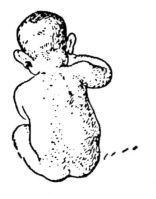

in this manner about seven times. Roll lightly, cut into strips, and make into twists or figure 8's or any other desired shape.

Place on a greased baking sheet and let rise in a warm room or on top of stove. Brush with melted butter and bake about 8 to 10 minutes at 400°. Brush with a powdered sugar icing while still hot; decorate with sliced almonds.

Illustration from: Ett Hem, *1899*

43

Danish Peppernuts
Pebernødder

1 cup butter
1/2 cup sugar
1/3 cup powdered sugar
1 egg

2 1/2 cups flour
1 teaspoon ginger
1 teaspoon ground cloves

Beat butter and sugars together until batter is well-blended and smooth. Beat in egg. Add flour and spices and mix well. Refrigerate dough for about 2 hours. Shape dough into 3/4-inch balls and place on a greased baking sheet. Bake at 300° for about 10 minutes, or until golden brown. Makes about 5 dozen.

Note: This traditional Scandinavian cookie is often placed in little woven-paper, heart-shaped baskets and hung on the tree at Christmas.

Danish Tea Cakes

1/2 cup butter
1 1/4 cups brown sugar, divided
1 cup flour + 2 tablespoons, divided
1/2 teaspoon baking powder
1/8 teaspoon salt

1/2 cup chopped nuts
1 1/2 cups coconut
2 eggs
1 teaspoon almond extract

Combine butter with 1/2 cup brown sugar and 1 cup of flour. Spread on a lightly greased cookie sheet. Bake at 350° for 10 minutes. In a small bowl, sift 2 tablespoons flour, the baking powder, and the salt over the nuts and coconut. Stir to coat, then spread on top of baked crust. In another bowl, beat eggs and add 3/4 cup brown sugar and almond extract; beat until light and fluffy. Mix well and spread over the layer of nuts and coconut. Bake 20 minutes in a 350° oven. Cool and cut into bars.

Finnish Cardamon Cookies

1 cup flour
1/4 teaspoon baking soda
1 teaspoon ground cinnamon
1 teaspoon ground cardamon

1 egg
3/4 cup white sugar
1/2 cup butter, melted

Mix flour, baking soda, cinnamon, and cardamon together in large bowl. Beat egg until frothy in second bowl; add sugar and butter. Mix well and add to dry ingredients. Mix until batter is smooth. Drop by teaspoonful onto greased and floured cookie sheet. Bake in 350° oven for 10 to 12 minutes or until brown. Makes about 5 dozen cookies.

Finnish Star Cookies

Date Filling:
1 cup sugar
1/2 pound dates, finely cut
1 cup water

Dough:
1 cup butter, softened and divided
1 1/2 cups flour
1/2 cup water
Cream and sugar for topping

Filling: Mix ingredients together and cook slowly until thickened. Cool.

Dough: Mix 1/2 cup of the butter with the flour. Add water slowly to make a smooth dough. When well mixed, chill dough. On a floured surface, roll out to 1/8 inch thickness. Spread half of the rolled-out dough with some (about 1/3) of the remaining butter; fold over buttered half and roll again to 1/8 inch thickness. Repeat until all butter is used. Then roll dough out until thin. Cut in 2 1/2-inch squares. Cut a 1-inch slash in each corner. Place a spoonful of date mixture in the center of each square. Fold opposite corners to center of filling. Brush with cream and sprinkle with sugar. Bake at 375° for 5 to 7 minutes. Makes about 5 dozen.

Gingerbread Cookies
Norwegian

1 cup butter
3/4 cup sugar
2/3 cup dark corn syrup
2-3 tablespoons cinnamon
1 teaspoon ground cloves

1 teaspoon ground cardamon
1 tablespoon ground ginger
1 teaspoon baking soda
1 cup chopped almonds
4 cups flour, divided

Prepare dough a day in advance. Melt butter in large pan over low heat. Remove from heat. Add sugar, syrup, spices, baking soda, almonds, and about 3 cups flour. Knead dough on floured board until smooth. Work in remaining flour. Roll dough into rolls, 2 inches in diameter. Chill overnight. Slice rolls into thin cookies. Bake on greased cookie sheet at 350° for 10 to 12 minutes. Makes about 12 dozen.

—*Royal Norwegian Embassy, Washington, D.C.*

Half-Moons
Icelandic

5 cups flour
2 3/4 cups butter
1 1/4 cups sugar
2 eggs

1 teaspoon hartshorn salt
1 teaspoon baking powder
2 teaspoons ground cardamon
Prune jam

Mix all ingredients, except jam, together in large bowl. When well-mixed, chill until firm. Remove from refrigerator and roll out dough to about 1/8 inch thickness. Cut out small rounds. Place 1/2 teaspoon prune jam on each round. Fold and, using a fork, press edges firmly together. Place the half-moons onto a greased baking sheet. Bake for 10 to 15 minutes at 350°. Makes about 5 dozen. This is a traditional Christmas recipe.

—Dua Clemensen, Independence, Missouri

Icelandic Cookies

1 cup sugar
1/2 cup butter
3 eggs (reserve 1 egg white)
1/2 cup milk

2 teaspoons caraway seeds
3 1/2 cups flour
3 teaspoons baking powder
1/2 teaspoon salt

Mix the sugar, butter, and eggs well. Add milk and caraway seeds. Sift together flour, baking powder, and salt and add to mixture to make a rather stiff dough. Roll pieces of dough into pencil-like strips about 8 inches long and form into the shape of pretzels. Place on greased cookie sheet. Brush with slightly beaten egg white. Bake at 350° for 10 to 12 minutes, or until golden brown. Makes 5 or 6 dozen.

—Evelyn Einarson Holand, Minot, North Dakota

Icelandic Fried Crullers
Asa's Kleinur

1 cup brown sugar
1 cup white sugar
2 eggs, beaten
1 cup buttermilk
1/2 cup cream

2 teaspoons ground cardamon
1 teaspoon baking soda
2 teaspoons baking powder
1 teaspoon salt
5 to 6 cups flour
Oil for frying

Combine first five ingredients. Stir together cardamon, baking soda, baking powder, salt, and 5 cups flour. Add to buttermilk mixture with enough flour to make soft dough. Turn onto floured surface and roll out to 1/4 inch thickness. Cut into 1x3-inch strips. Cut a slit in center of strip. Twist one end of strip through the hole. Heat oil for deep-frying, as if for doughnuts, and fry *Kleinur* until golden brown. Makes about 6 dozen.

Icelandic Rolled Cookies

2/3 cup sugar
1 cup butter, softened
1 1/4 to 2 cups flour, divided

1/2 teaspoon baking powder
1 egg yolk, beaten
Sugar for sprinkling

Cream sugar and butter together. Combine 1 1/4 cups of flour and the baking powder; add to butter mixture. Mix well. Use remaining flour to prepare floured surface, then roll out dough and cut into desired shapes. Place cookies on a greased baking sheet. Brush with egg yolk and sprinkle with sugar. Bake at 350° for 10 to 12 minutes, or until lightly browned. Makes about 4 dozen cookies.

—*Fred Bjornson, Cedar Rapids, Iowa*

Krumbles
Finnish

Dough:
1 cup brown sugar
1 cup margarine, softened
1 egg

1 teaspoon vanilla
2 cups flour
2 cups oatmeal

Topping:
8 ounces dates, chopped
3/4 cup sugar

2 tablespoons water

Dough: Mix all ingredients together. Put 3/4 of the dough on a 10x15-inch jelly roll pan. Pat into place and prepare topping.

Topping: Mix together all ingredients. Bring to a boil and cook about 2 to 3 minutes.

Assembly: Cover dough with topping mixture. Crumble remaining dough over date topping. Bake about 15 to 20 minutes at 350°. Cool and cut into bars.

Macaroons

Danish

1/2 pound almond paste
1 cup white sugar
3 egg whites
1/3 cup powdered sugar
Chocolate, melted

Break almond paste into small pieces. Add sugar and mix well. Add egg whites and beat until well-blended. Stir in powdered sugar. Shape with a pastry tube on lightly greased cookie sheets. Bake in a 350° oven for 12 to 15 minutes until macaroons are golden brown. Dip into melted chocolate when cool. Makes about 5 dozen.

54

Drawing from: Larssons, *1902*

Mocha Squares
Finnish

Marja, my cousin, says this is a family favorite in my parents' hometown of Vaasa.

3 eggs
2 cups sugar
1 cup lukewarm milk
1 cup butter, melted

3 1/3 cups flour
3 tablespoons cocoa powder
3 teaspoons baking powder
3 teaspoons vanilla sugar

Icing:
2 cups powdered sugar
6 tablespoons melted butter
6 tablespoons hot coffee

2 tablespoons cocoa powder
2 tablespoons vanilla sugar

Beat together eggs and sugar. Add milk and butter. Mix in other ingredients. Pour into greased large jelly roll pan. Bake at 425° for about 15 minutes, or until done.
Icing: Mix all ingredients and pour over hot cake. Decorate with coconut flakes, chocolate chips, or small candies. Cut into squares.

—*Marja Lybeck-Pesonen, Vaasa, Finland*

Norwegian Butter Rings

Berlinerkranser

2 hard-cooked egg yolks
2 large eggs, separated
1/2 cup granulated sugar

2 cups flour
1 cup butter, softened
Pearl sugar (found in most food
    specialty shops)

In a large bowl, mash the hard-cooked egg yolks; add the raw yolks and the granulated sugar. Beat mixture with an electric mixer until it is light and fluffy. Add flour and butter alternately to mixture, beating well after each addition. Chill dough overnight. Roll 1 tablespoon of dough into a 4 1/2-inch rope. Form the rope into a wreath ring, overlapping the ends, and transfer to a greased baking sheet. Make wreath rings with the remaining dough in the same manner and arrange them 2 inches apart on baking sheet. Beat egg whites until they are frothy and brush tops of rings; sprinkle with pearl sugar and bake at 350° for 10 to 12 minutes until golden brown. Cool on cookie sheets for 1 minute; transfer to racks to cool completely.

Norwegian Cookies
Kringla

1 1/2 cups sugar
1 egg, beaten
2 cups sour cream
1 teaspoon vanilla

4 cups sifted flour
2 teaspoons baking soda
1/4 teaspoon salt

Mix sugar, egg, sour cream, and vanilla; beat well. Mix in sifted flour, soda, and salt. Cover the dough and refrigerate overnight. On a board, with the palms of your hands, roll a small amount of dough pencil-thin and about 8 inches long; form a figure 8. Place cookies on a lightly floured cookie sheet. Bake at 375° for 12 minutes, until light golden in color. Makes 6 to 7 dozen. Store in airtight container.

Norwegian Cookies
Sandbakkels

1 cup butter	1 tablespoon brandy
1 cup margarine	(or brandy flavoring)
1 cup sugar	1 egg
6 tablespoons whipping cream	6 cups flour

Cream butter, margarine, and sugar. Add cream, brandy, and egg. Slowly add flour until all is well-mixed. Chill slightly before pressing into *Sandbakkel* tins. Roll into small balls. Press into tins and keep pressing until thin layer covers bottom and sides. Trim off excess from edges. Bake at 350° until light golden in color. Makes 5 dozen.

Note: You can purchase *Sandbakkel* tins at Scandinavian specialty shops.

—*Lois Wold Christenson, Decorah, Iowa*
From: Notably Norwegian: Recipes, Festivals, Folk Arts

Norwegian Fried Cookies
Fattigmand

4 egg yolks
4 tablespoons sugar
4 tablespoons cream
4 tablespoons butter, melted
1 tablespoon lemon juice

2 cups flour
1/2 teaspoon ground cardamon
Oil for deep-frying
Powdered sugar for sprinkling

Beat egg yolks until light and fluffy. Add sugar, cream, melted butter, and lemon juice. Beat well. Stir in flour and cardamon; mix well to form a smooth dough. Roll dough out into thin sheets on lightly floured pastry cloth. Cut into diamond shapes, then cut a slit in the center of each diamond and pull one corner through. Deep-fry in hot oil, about 350°, until brown. Drain on paper towel. When cool, sprinkle with powdered sugar.

Norwegian Raisin Cookies

1/2 cup butter
1 cup sugar
2 eggs
4 tablespoons half-and-half
3 1/2 cups flour

1 teaspoon soda
1/4 teaspoon ginger
1 teaspoon cinnamon (optional)
1 teaspoon vanilla
3/4 cup raisins, chopped

Topping:
1 egg white, beaten
4 tablespoons sugar
1 teaspoon half-and-half

5 tablespoons finely chopped almonds
1 teaspoon cinnamon (optional)

Cream butter and sugar until well blended. Add eggs and half-and-half; beat well. Add flour that has been sifted with soda and spices. Add vanilla and chopped raisins. Chill dough overnight. When ready to bake, roll small pieces of dough into 2-inch strips. Form wreaths. **Topping:** Beat ingredients together and spread on top of each cookie. Bake at 350° for 10 to 12 minutes. Makes 6 to 7 dozen.

Norwegian Spritz

1 cup butter or margarine
2/3 cup sugar
3 egg yolks

1 teaspoon almond extract
1/2 teaspoon vanilla extract
2 1/2 cups flour

Also needed: Cookie press

Cream butter or margarine and sugar. Add egg yolks and extracts. Mix well. Add flour and mix well. Press dough onto cookie sheets through cookie press into different designs. Bake at 350° for 10 to 12 minutes until light golden brown. Makes about 6 dozen.

—Irene O. Engebretson, Decorah, Iowa
From: Notably Norwegian: Recipes, Festivals, Folk Arts

Norwegian Wafer Cones

Krumkake

1 cup melted butter	1/2 teaspoon salt
1 cup sugar	2 cups flour
3 eggs	1/2 teaspoon grated lemon rind
1 cup cream	1/2 teaspoon lemon juice

Mix all ingredients together in a large bowl. If dough will not hold together, add a little milk to the mixture. Place about 1 to 2 tablespoons of the batter in a hot *krumkake* iron and bake until each side is light golden brown (about 30 seconds on each side). Remove from iron and quickly roll the *kake* around wooden cone-shaped baking stick to form the cone shape. Place seam side down on waxed paper to cool. Remove form. Cooled cones may be filled with sweetened whipped cream, if desired.

Prune Tarts
Finnish

Pastry:
2 cups butter, divided
4 cups all-purpose flour
3/4 cup cold water

Filling:
1 pound prunes, stewed and pitted
1/2 cup sugar

Pastry:
Cut 1 cup of the butter into the flour until mixture resembles coarse crumbs. Add the water and combine to form dough. Chill 30 minutes, then roll out and dot with 1/4 cup butter. Fold dough from front toward back, from back to front, and from each side toward center. Chill again. Repeat process of rolling and chilling, adding dots of butter (about 1/4 cup) three times, or until all butter is used. Roll again. Cut into 3-inch squares. Cut a slit in each corner of each square.

continued

Prune Tarts *continued*

Filling: Drain prunes and mix with sugar.

Assembly: Place a spoonful of prune filling in the center of each square. Turn up alternating corners (as in making a pinwheel) and pinch together in the center. Chill. Bake at 400° for 13 to 15 minutes, or until golden brown. Cool and serve. Makes 5 to 6 dozen.

—*Dorothy Tamminen, Pengilly, Minnesota*
From: Scandinavian Christmas:
Recipes and Traditions

Rosettes
Norwegian

2 large eggs
2 tablespoons white sugar
1 cup milk
1 cup flour

1/4 teaspoon salt (optional)
Vegetable oil
Powdered sugar

In a bowl, beat together the eggs and the sugar until well blended. Add milk, flour, and salt and beat again until mixture is smooth. In a deep-fat cooker or electric frypan, heat oil until it registers about 370° on a deep-fat thermometer. Dip rosette iron into batter, being careful not to let the batter cover the top of the iron. Fry the batter adhering to the iron in the oil for 30 to 40 seconds, or until golden brown. Raise iron, allowing excess oil to drop off, and with a fork gently pry rosette from iron onto paper toweling to drain. Repeat process for each rosette. When cool, sift powdered sugar over the rosettes. Store in airtight container. Makes about 3 dozen.

Runeberg Tarts

Finnish

This traditional Finnish delicacy was created for J. L. Runeberg, Finland's national poet.

1 egg
1 cup sugar
1/2 cup plus 3 tablespoons butter, melted and cooled
1/2 cup plus 3 tablespoons sour cream

1 teaspoon almond flavoring
2 cups flour
2 teaspoons cinnamon
2 teaspoons baking powder

Filling:

1/4 cup powdered sugar
Little water

Yellow food coloring
Strawberry jam

Tarts: Beat egg and sugar together until light and fluffy. Fold in cooled melted butter, sour cream, and almond flavoring. Mix dry ingredients and add to first mixture. Fill small muffin tins or tart shells half-full. Bake at 375° 12 to 15 minutes. **Topping:** Mix sugar, a little water, and coloring until thick and creamy. Put a little jam into each tart and, using a tube, decorate with icing. About 2 dozen tarts.

Scandinavian Pastry
Kringle

Pastry:
1 cup flour
1/2 cup chilled margarine

2 tablespoons cold water

Puff Topping:
1 cup water
1/2 cup margarine
1 cup flour

3 eggs
1 teaspoon almond flavoring

Frosting:
1 cup powdered sugar
1 tablespoon margarine

1 teaspoon almond flavoring
2 to 3 tablespoons milk
Chopped nuts (optional)

Pastry: With a pastry blender, cut together flour and margarine until crumbly. Sprinkle water over mixture; mix with a fork until well blended. Divide dough in half. On an ungreased cookie sheet, press each half to form a 12x3-inch strip. Heat oven to 350°.

67

continued

Scandinavian Pastry *continued*

Puff Topping: In a saucepan, heat water and margarine until boiling. Remove from heat and stir in flour. Add eggs one at a time, beating after each until smooth. Add almond flavoring; spoon over strips. Bake for 50 minutes. Frost while warm.

Frosting: Blend powdered sugar, margarine, almond flavoring, and milk until smooth. Drizzle over *Kringle*. Sprinkle with nuts if desired. Cut and serve.

—*Ruth Willmes, Dollar Bay, Michigan*

Illustration from: Ett Hem, *1899*

Swedish Coffee Fingers

1 1/2 cups soft butter
1 cup sugar
1 egg yolk
1 teaspoon almond extract

4 cups flour (approximate)
1 egg white, slightly beaten
Nuts, chopped fine

Cream butter and sugar until fluffy. Add egg yolk and almond extract. Add flour, until mixture is easily handled. Form into roll, wrap in waxed paper, and refrigerate as for icebox cookies. Chill dough until firm enough to slice thin. Brush each cookie with slightly beaten egg white and sprinkle with chopped nuts. Bake at 350° for 15 to 18 minutes or until cookies are slightly browned. Makes about 15 dozen.

—Clarence Nelson, East Lansing, Michigan

Swedish Cookies

1/2 cup shortening
1/2 cup butter or margarine, softened
1 cup sifted powdered sugar
1/2 teaspoon salt
2 cups flour

1 tablespoon water
1 tablespoon vanilla extract
3/4 cup ground peanuts
Powdered sugar

Cream shortening and butter or margarine. Add powdered sugar and salt; mix well. Blend in flour. Stir in water, vanilla, and peanuts. Shape dough into 1-inch balls. Place on ungreased baking sheets. Flatten slightly. Bake at 325° for 12-15 minutes. Remove from oven and dip into powdered sugar. Makes about 5 dozen.

—Elsie Fretter, Dollar Bay, Michigan

Swedish Dreams
Drömmar

1/2 cup butter or margarine
1/3 cup sugar
1 cup all-purpose flour

1 teaspoon vanilla sugar
1/2 teaspoon *hjorthornssalt*
(ammonium carbonate)

Stir butter and sugar until very light in color and thickened. Add flour, vanilla sugar, and *hjorthornssalt* and stir into the butter-sugar mixture. Chill dough in refrigerator for about 15 minutes. Form dough into small, round balls, about 1 inch in diameter. Bake on ungreased cookie sheet in a 350° oven for 15 to 20 minutes. If *Drömmar* appears to be browning too fast, reduce oven temperature. (There may be a little smell of ammonia while baking.) Makes about 4 dozen.

Note: Ammonium carbonate can be found in some drugstores, or specialty shops such as Anderson Butik's Swedish Timber Cottage in Lindsborg, Kansas. Vanilla sugar is also available at Anderson's; however, 1 teaspoon liquid vanilla may be substituted for 1 teaspoon vanilla sugar. —*Charlotte J. Anderson, Lindsborg, Kansas*

Swedish Ginger Cookies
Pepparkakor

1 cup butter
1 1/2 cups white sugar
1 tablespoon white corn syrup
1 large egg
1 teaspoon soda

2 teaspoons cinnamon
2 teaspoons ginger
1 scant teaspoon cloves
2 1/2 cups white flour (sifted)

Cream butter together with sugar and corn syrup until smooth. Add egg and beat well. Stir in soda, cinnamon, ginger, and cloves. Fold in flour. Add more flour as needed, to make dough easy to handle. Roll dough onto floured board with rolling pin to about 1/4 inch thickness. Cut into heart shapes. Place on ungreased cookie sheet and bake for 7 to 10 minutes in a 350° oven. Remove from pan when cool and store in airtight containers.
—*Catrine Kostenius-Foster, Lulea, Sweden*

Swedish Sugar Twists
Småland Kringlor

1 egg
1 cup sugar
1/2 cup thick sour cream
1 teaspoon soda
1 teaspoon almond or vanilla flavoring

1 tablespoon butter, melted
2 1/2 cups flour (or enough to roll)
1/2 teaspoon baking powder
Pinch of salt

Whip egg in a large bowl. Add sugar and mix well. Add sour cream and soda and mix again. Add flavoring and butter. Work in flour, baking powder, and salt until dough is smooth. On a floured surface, roll dough into strips, about 7 inches long and pencil-thin. Shape like a pretzel. Place on greased cookie sheet and bake in preheated 350° oven for 8 to 10 minutes until golden brown in color. About 4 dozen.

—*Ruby Johnson, Lansing, Michigan*

Swedish Wedding Cookies
Giftas

3 eggs
3/4 cup powdered sugar
1 cup flour

Whipped cream
Preserves (lingonberry, raspberry)

Preheat oven to 475°. Beat eggs and the sugar together. Slowly stir in flour; beat well. Spread a little flour on a cookie sheet. Spread spoonfuls of batter on cookie sheet in circles, about the size of a saucer. Bake about 10 to 12 minutes or until golden brown. Remove from oven and remove *Giftas* from cookie sheet carefully with a spatula. While they are still soft, form them into cones and allow them to cool and harden. Combine whipped cream and preserves and fill the cones. Serve immediately. Makes about 4 dozen.

White Christmas Cookies
Finnish

1 cup sugar
1 cup butter
2 eggs
3 tablespoons cream
1 teaspoon vanilla

3 cups flour, sifted
1/4 teaspoon salt
1 teaspoon baking soda
1/2 teaspoon cream of tartar

Blend the sugar and butter together. Add the eggs, cream, and vanilla. Add the sifted flour, salt, soda, and cream of tartar. Chill dough in refrigerator at least 1 hour before rolling out thin on floured board. Using holiday cookie cutters, cut out cookies. Place on lightly greased cookie sheet and bake at 375° for 7 to 10 minutes. Makes about 5 dozen cookies. —*Shirlyn Bentley, New York Mills, Minnesota*

Almond Tosca Cake
Norwegian

Batter:

3 eggs	1 1/2 teaspoons baking powder
1 cup sugar	1/4 cup butter, melted
1 teaspoon vanilla	3 tablespoons milk
1 1/2 cups flour	

Topping:

1/3 cup butter	1/2 cup whipped cream
1/2 cup slivered, blanched almonds	4 ounces shredded gjetost cheese
1/2 cup sugar	

Beat eggs until foamy. Add sugar and beat until light and lemon-colored. Add vanilla. Mix flour with baking powder and fold into the egg mixture until blended.

continued

Almond Tosca Cake *continued*

Mix butter and milk and stir into the flour-egg mixture until batter is well blended. Turn into a buttered 10-inch springform pan with a removable bottom. Bake at 350° for 35 minutes.

Topping: Melt butter in frying pan. Add almonds, stirring until golden brown. Stir in sugar and cream; bring to a vigorous boil, stirring constantly. Boil for 2 1/2 minutes, until mixture becomes caramel-colored and thickens slightly. Stir in gjetost and continue stirring until smooth. Pour hot topping over cake and place under broiler until topping is bubbly and lightly browned. Cut into eight slices and serve.

—*Royal Norwegian Embassy, Washington, D.C.*

Apple Cake
Norwegian

1/2 cup shortening
2 cups sugar, divided
2 eggs, beaten
1 teaspoon vanilla
2 1/2 cups flour

1 teaspoon salt
2 teaspoons baking powder
1 cup milk
Peeled, cored, and sliced apples
2 teaspoons cinnamon

Cream shortening and 1 cup of sugar together. Add beaten eggs and vanilla to mixture. Add dry ingredients alternately with the milk. Spread in a 13x9-inch greased and floured pan. Top with apple slices. Mix cinnamon and 1 cup sugar; sprinkle over the top. Bake at 350° for 30 to 45 minutes.

—*Pearl Jalkanen, Hancock, Michigan*

Christmas Cake
Icelandic

1 cup margarine
8 tablespoons sugar
2-3 eggs
4 cups flour

1 teaspoon ground cardamon
2 teaspoons baking powder
3/4 cup milk
3 tablespoons raisins

Cream margarine and sugar until light and fluffy. Add eggs, one at a time, mixing well. Mix together flour, cardamon, and baking powder and add alternately with the milk. Add raisins. Pour batter into a greased 9x5-inch loaf pan. Cover with waxed paper and bake at 300° for 1 hour. Remove paper and continue baking for another 30 minutes until done.
—*Dua Clemensen, Independence, Missouri*

Icelandic Cake

1/2 cup butter, softened
1 cup plus 1 tablespoon sugar
1 cup milk
2 1/2 cups flour

2 1/2 teaspoons baking powder
2 cups raisins
dash of ground cardamon
3 egg whites, well-beaten

Cream butter and sugar together. Slowly add milk, flour, and baking powder. Add raisins and cardamon and beat well. Fold in well-beaten egg whites. Pour batter into a 13x9x2-inch pan and bake at 350° for about 45 minutes, or until cake tests done.

Icelandic Torte

1/2 cup margarine
1/2 cup shortening
2 cups sugar
4 eggs
1/2 cup sour cream
1 teaspoon vanilla
Filling:
3 pounds pitted prunes
Water to cover prunes
2 cups sugar

6 cups flour
1 teaspoon soda
1 teaspoon baking powder
1 teaspoon ground cardamon

1 teaspoon ground cardamon
1 tablespoon lemon juice

Cream shortenings and sugar. Beat in eggs, one at a time. Add sour cream and vanilla. Mix and add dry ingredients. Mix until dough is stiff. Divide into 12 balls. Roll each

continued

Icelandic Torte *continued*

ball out on lightly floured pastry cloth. Place dinner plate on dough and cut around it. Transfer to a cookie sheet and bake at 350° for 10 to 12 minutes or until golden brown. You will have 12 large cookies which will make two six-layer cakes.

Filling: Place prunes in saucepan. Cover with water and boil until prunes are tender and water is absorbed. Add sugar, cardamon, and lemon juice. Spread between layers of two cakes, about 1/2 cup of prunes between each layer.

—Evelyn Einarson Holand, Minot, North Dakota

Ida's Orange Fruit Cake
Swedish

Rind of 1 orange
1 cup raisins
1 cup sugar
1/2 cup butter
2 eggs
Glaze:
Juice of 1 orange

1 teaspoon vanilla
2 cups flour
1 teaspoon soda
2/3 cup sour milk
1/2 cup chopped nuts

1/2 cup powdered sugar

Put orange rind and raisins through a grinder or food chopper. Set aside. Cream sugar and butter together. Add eggs and vanilla; beat well. Sift dry ingredients together and add to butter mixture alternately with sour milk. Fold in orange-raisin mixture and nuts and pour mixture into well-greased tube pan.

83

continued

Ida's Orange Fruit Cake *continued*

Bake in a preheated 350° oven for 1 hour or until a toothpick inserted into cake comes out clean. Turn cake onto a rack to cool.

Glaze:
Mix together orange juice and powdered sugar. When cake has cooled, pour or brush glaze over hot cake.

—*Carol Bostrom Neuman, Lansing, Michigan*

My mother and Ida Bostrom, Carol's mother, became good friends in 1928 when my mother emigrated from Finland to the United States. Along with a few other families they comprised one of the first close-knit Scandinavian communities in Lansing. They met frequently for afternoon coffee and Scandinavian parties to share the news they received from the Old Country. —*Karen Berg Douglas*

Jarlsberg Coffee Cake
Norwegian

1 cup sugar
3 cups sifted flour
2 teaspoons baking powder
1/2 teaspoon salt
1/4 teaspoon nutmeg
1/2 cup butter, softened
2 eggs

1/2 cup milk
1/2 cup chopped walnuts
1/2 cup chopped apples
1 tablespoon lemon juice
2 cups Jarslberg cheese, diced
1 teaspoon cinnamon
2 tablespoons sugar

Combine sugar, flour, baking powder, salt, and nutmeg. Add softened butter. Add eggs, milk, and nuts, then apples, lemon juice, and cheese. Pour into an 8x8-inch greased baking pan. Sprinkle cinnamon and sugar on top. Bake at 350° for 30 to 35 minutes.

Lingonberry Cake
Finnish

1/4 cup butter (or margarine)
1 cup sugar, divided
1 large egg
1 cup white flour

1 teaspoon baking powder
1/8 teaspoon salt
1 1/2 cups preserved lingonberries
Whipped cream for topping

Preheat oven to 350°. In a large bowl, cream together butter and 3/4 cup of sugar until smooth. Add egg and continue beating until mixture is smooth and thick. In a separate bowl, sift together flour, baking powder, and salt. Gradually add flour mixture to first mixture, and stir until smooth. Pour batter into a buttered 13x9x2-inch baking pan and spread evenly. Top batter with lingonberries and sprinkle with 1/4 cup sugar. Bake for about 30 minutes until brown at edges. Serve warm topped with a dab of whipped cream.

Midsummer Dreams
Swedish

3 eggs
3/4 cup sugar
1 cup flour
Filling:
3 tablespoons sugar

1 teaspoon baking powder
1/4 cup almonds, chopped
Sugar for sprinkling on top

2 cups strawberries, mashed

Preheat oven to 450°. Line a 12x15-inch baking tin with baking or parchment paper. Beat eggs and sugar together until light and fluffy. Mix flour, baking powder, and chopped almonds together; fold carefully into the sugar and egg mixtures. Spread batter in the baking pan. Bake for about 5 minutes and remove from oven. Sprinkle sugar onto the warm finished cake and carefully turn it over onto a second sheet of parchment paper,

continued

Midsummer Dreams *continued*

sugared side down. Remove top sheet of parchment paper. If it won't loosen easily, brush with a little cold water.

Filling and assembly: Stir sugar into the mashed strawberries; spread mixture onto the cake. Roll up the cake from the long side and allow it to cool with the seam side down. Place roll on a tray lined with parchment paper and refrigerate for several hours before serving. Cut into 1-inch-thick slices to serve. Garnish with whipped cream and sliced strawberries. Serves 10.

Drawing from: Ett Hem, *1899*

Norwegian Ring Tree Cake
Kransekake

1 pound almond paste
1 pound powdered sugar, sifted

2 egg whites, unbeaten
1/4 cup powdered sugar for kneading

Mix almond paste and 1 pound powdered sugar. Add egg whites. Mix well. Place bowl in hot water and knead dough until it is lukewarm. Turn out on board sprinkled with 1/4 cup powdered sugar. Let rest 10 minutes. Knead 2 to 3 minutes. Press dough through cookie press into greased, graduated ring forms. Bake at 300° for 20 minutes. Do not remove rings from forms until cold. Place rings on top of one another, icing each one with frosting as you stack them.

Frosting:

1 1/2 cups powdered sugar, sifted

1 egg white
1 teaspoon vinegar

Mix well and drizzle over all cake rings. Decorate with small Norwegian flags.

continued

Ring Tree Cake *continued*

The *Kransekake,* or Ring Tree Cake, is a festival tradition in Norway. It is served at Christmas because of its tree shape, at weddings because of its impressive height, and for anniversaries and birthdays because of its many layers. It can be made in as many rings as there are years to celebrate.

—*Arla Erickson Lyon, Decorah, Iowa*
From: Notably Norwegian: Recipes, Festivals, Folk Arts

Note: The icing used to assemble this cake calls for uncooked eggs. If you wish to heed the caution on the consumption of uncooked eggs, we suggest using a prepared commercial glaze as a substitute.

Sportscake
Danish

This was named after the 1891 comedy "Sportsmen." The cast from Copenhagen's famous Folk Theater ordered it regularly. It consists of a macaroon base, whipped cream with crushed caramel, and caramel-dipped puff pastries.

Macaroon base:

3 1/2 ounces almond paste

1 cup sugar

2 or 3 egg whites

Mix almond paste and sugar together. Add egg whites and blend to a porridge-like consistency. Spread onto large, round baking sheet, such as a pizza tin. Bake 20 minutes at 350°.

continued

Sportscake *continued*

Puff Pastries:

4 cups water	4 cups flour
1 pound plus 3 tablespoons butter	17 eggs

Bring water and butter to a boil. Stir continuously. Add flour and continue to boil until mixture comes away from saucepan. Cool. Stir in eggs until there is a smooth consistency. Form into 24 quarter-sized pieces; place about 1 1/2 inches apart on a lightly greased cookie sheet. Bake for 20 to 30 minutes at 400°.

Whipped cream with crushed caramel:

2 cups powdered sugar	4 cups whipped cream
1 cup crushed almonds	

Heat powdered sugar, using a double boiler, until there is a liquid consistency. Dip baked puff pastries into mixture. Take remaining mixture and add almonds until it is
continued

Sportscake *continued*

a golden brown, caramel-like color. Spread mixture onto a cookie sheet and cool. Cover end of a hammer with cloth and crush hardened mixture into crumbs. Mix whipped cream and crushed caramel mixture into firm consistency.

Assembly:
Spoon whipped cream and crushed caramel over the macaroon base like a half-ball. (After all, it is a Sportscake!) Put the puff pastries dipped in caramel on the edge of the cake in two circular rows. Pipe the Sportscake with whipped cream; this can be accomplished by using an icing bag with a flat spout.

—*Conditoriet La Glace, Copenhagen, Denmark*

Strawberry Torte
Finnish

2 quarts fresh strawberries, divided
1 teaspoon lemon juice
4 eggs, separated
1/4 cup sugar

12 coconut cookies (or vanilla wafers), crushed
Whipped cream (optional)

Preheat oven to 350°. Mash about 3/4 of the strawberries in large bowl. Add 1 teaspoon lemon juice. Beat egg yolks and sugar in a separate bowl until light in color. Add the crushed strawberries and crushed cookies to egg yolk mixture. Beat egg whites until stiff. Fold egg whites into mixture carefully. Pour mixture into a buttered two-quart baking dish and bake for about 30 minutes, or until firm. Serve cold with remaining strawberries, whole or sliced. Top with whipped cream, if desired.

Swedish Cheese Cake
Ostkaka

8 quarts whole milk	6 eggs
1 1/3 cups flour	1 quart heavy whipping cream
3 drops liquid rennet	1/2 cup sugar
1/4 cup cold water	Pinch of salt

Heat milk to lukewarm. Mix flour with a little milk and add to warm milk. Dissolve rennet in cold water and stir into milk mixture. Stir milk over low heat until it curdles and turns into cheese. Put into a colander and strain until the whey, or water, is gone. Beat eggs with cream, sugar, and salt and mix with cheese. Pour into 10x14-inch baking pan and bake for 1 1/2 hours at 325°. Serve with raspberry jam for dessert.

Swedish Ginger Cake
Mjuk Pepparkaka

1/2 cup butter or margarine, melted
   and divided
Fine dry bread crumbs
2 eggs
1 1/4 cups sugar
1 1/4 cups all-purpose flour

1 1/2 teaspoons baking powder
2 teaspoons ground cinnamon
1 teaspoon ground cardamon
1 teaspoon ground ginger (optional)
1 teaspoon ground cloves (optional)
2/3 cup milk or half-and-half

Using about 1 tablespoon butter, butter an angel food cake pan or round pan that will hold about 6 to 7 cups. Then sprinkle the pan with fine dry bread crumbs. Beat eggs and sugar until pale and thick and mixture starts to bubble. Mix flour, baking powder, and spices together thoroughly. Stir the flour mixture into the egg mixture. Add the melted butter and milk. Stir to a smooth batter. Pour into buttered pan and bake 50 to 60 minutes at 350°. Cake is done when toothpick inserted in center comes out clean.

—Charlotte J. Anderson, Lindsborg, Kansas

Swedish Torte

6 tablespoons butter or margarine	4 ounces almonds, ground fine
1 cup sugar	3 egg whites, beaten stiff
1 cup milk	

Vanilla sauce topping:

4 tablespoons sugar	3 tablespoons butter
3 egg yolks	1 tablespoon vanilla
1 cup half-and-half	Whipped cream, red cherries (optional)

Mix butter, sugar, milk, and almonds together. Fold in beaten egg whites. Pour into greased 8-inch round cake pan. Bake at 325° for 30 minutes.

Vanilla sauce: Mix all ingredients together and cook in a double boiler over hot water until thickened. Remove from heat; pour into a bowl and chill in the refrigerator, stirring occasionally. Spoon over cooled cake. Top with whipped cream and red cherries for a festive dessert.

Butterscotch Dessert

Pastry:

1/2 cup margarine

1 cup flour

Filling:

1/2 cup powdered sugar

1 8-ounce package cream cheese

2 cups milk

3/4 cup finely chopped walnuts

2 tablespoons sugar

2 3-ounce packages instant
  butterscotch pudding

Whipped cream

Pastry: Combine all ingredients and pat into 9x13x2-inch pan. Bake 15 minutes at 350°. Cool.

Filling: Cream powdered sugar and cream cheese. Spread over crust. Mix milk and butterscotch pudding. Cool. Spread over cream cheese mixture. Place in refrigerator until firm. Top with whipped cream.

—Pearl Stoor, Dollar Bay, Michigan

Cherry Cream Cheese Dessert

2 cups flour
1/2 cup brown sugar
1/4 cup margarine
1 cup pecans, chopped

1 8-ounce package cream cheese
1 cup powdered sugar
1/2 pint heavy cream, whipped
1 can cherry pie filling

Mix flour, brown sugar, margarine, and pecans and spread into 9x13x2-inch pan. Bake at 350° for 15 minutes. Remove from pan and crumble while warm. Cool. Reserve 1 cup crumbs for topping. Spread remaining crumbs in pan. Pat down. Beat cream cheese and powdered sugar together. Fold whipped cream into cream cheese mixture; spread on top of crumb crust. Top with cherry pie filling. Sprinkle with reserved crumbs. Refrigerate overnight and serve. *—Sigrid Tervonen, Escanaba, Michigan*
—Iris Burge, Dollar Bay, Michigan

Finnish Almond Brittle

1 cup butter or margarine, softened
1 1/2 cups powdered sugar
1 egg

1 teaspoon vanilla
2 1/2 cups flour
2 teaspoons almond extract

Mix butter, sugar, egg, and vanilla thoroughly. Blend in flour. Mix in almond extract. Cover; chill at least 2 hours. Heat oven to 375°. Roll dough 1/4 inch thick on a lightly floured board. Cut into strips, 2 1/2 inches x 3/4 inch. Bake on ungreased cookie sheet 10 to 12 minutes until very light brown. Cool. Makes 8 dozen. Frost with **holiday frosting** (following recipe).

Holiday Frosting

4 cups powdered sugar
1 teaspoon vanilla
1 1/2 tablespoons milk

Few drops of food coloring
2/3 cup blanched almonds, finely
chopped

Blend powdered sugar, vanilla, milk, and food coloring. If using different colors of food coloring, divide the frosting and blend a few drops into each part. Spread frosting on Finnish almond brittle. Sprinkle each piece with blanched almonds.

—Marlis Runnberg, Finland, Minnesota
From: Scandinavian Christmas Recipes and Traditions

Finnish Fruit Soup

1 1/2 pounds mixed dried fruit
(apricots, prunes, apples, raisins)
11 cups water
1 cinnamon stick

1 1/2 cups white sugar
2 tablespoons cornstarch
2 tablespoons cold water
Whipped cream (optional)

Simmer the dried fruits in the 11 cups of water with the cinnamon stick and sugar until fruit is tender, about 45 minutes to an hour. Mix the cornstarch into the 2 tablespoons cold water. Bring soup to boil and add cornstarch mixture. Continue cooking fruit soup over low heat until thick. Serve in glass cups. Top with whipped cream, if desired. About 8 to 10 servings.

Gevalia Coffee Ice Cream

3 cups light cream
1 1/4 cups sugar
3 beaten eggs
1/2 cup cold Gevalia Kaffe

Salt
1 cup heavy whipping cream
1 1/2 teaspoons vanilla
1/4 cup rum (optional)

Also needed: Electric or hand-operated ice cream freezer.

Scald light cream while blending in sugar. Add slowly to beaten eggs and blend thoroughly. Cook while stirring on top of a double boiler until thickened, then chill. Add the chilled Gevalia Kaffe, salt, and whipping cream to the chilled egg mixture. Begin churning in freezer. When almost frozen, add vanilla, and rum if desired.

—Gevalia Kaffe Import Service

Gjetost Bread Pudding
Norwegian

4 cups milk
4 eggs, divided
3/4 cup sugar, divided
2 teaspoons vanilla
1/4 teaspoon ground cinnamon

1/8 teaspoon salt
8 slices bread, cubed
1/2 cup golden raisins
1/2 cup shredded gjetost cheese
1/2 cup orange marmalade

In saucepan, heat milk until bubbles appear around edge of pan. Remove from heat. Separate two eggs; set whites aside. In bowl, blend two whole eggs, two egg yolks, 1/2 cup sugar, vanilla, cinnamon, and salt. Gradually beat in milk. In buttered 1 1/2 quart baking dish, combine bread, raisins, and cheese. Pour egg mixture over all. Bake at 325° for 50 minutes or until knife inserted into center comes out clean. Remove from oven.

continued

Gjetost Bread Pudding *continued*

Carefully spread marmalade on top of pudding. Beat egg whites until foamy. Gradually beat in remaining 1/4 cup sugar until mixture holds stiff peaks. Spread over marmalade, sealing meringue to edges of dish. Bake 10 minutes longer or until meringue is golden brown. Serve warm or cold. Makes 6 to 8 servings.

Gjetost Peach Cobbler

Fruit mixture:
4 cups peeled, sliced fresh peaches
1/3 cup sugar
1 cup water
1/4 cup orange juice
1/4 cup butter or margarine
1 1/2 tablespoons cornstarch
1/2 teaspoon ground cinnamon
1 tablespoon lemon juice

Batter:
3/4 cup flour
1/4 cup sugar
1 teaspoon baking powder
1/8 teaspoon salt
1 egg yolk
1/2 cup sour cream
1 tablespoon melted butter
1/4 teaspoon grated lemon peel
1 cup shredded gjetost cheese, divided

Fruit mixture: Sprinkle peaches with 1/3 cup sugar; set aside. In saucepan, combine water, orange juice, butter, cornstarch, cinnamon, and lemon juice. Cook, stirring until thickened and smooth. Add peaches; keep warm.

continued

Gjetost Peach Cobbler *continued*

In large bowl, combine remaining ingredients, except cheese. Stir just until combined. Stir in 1/2 cup cheese. Spoon hot peach mixture into 1 1/2 quart baking dish. Top with 1/2 cup cheese. Drop batter into six portions on top of peaches. Bake at 350° for 35 minutes, or until dumplings are golden brown. Serve warm with cream. Makes 6 servings.

Illustration from: Spadarvet, *1906*

Icelandic Pancakes with Whipped Cream

3 cups flour
4 egg yolks
2 1/2 to 3 cups milk
3 tablespoons melted butter
Topping:
Preserves, jam, or jelly

1/2 teaspoon baking soda
1/2 teaspoon baking powder
1 teaspoon vanilla essence
4 egg whites, stiffly beaten

Whipped cream

Beat together all ingredients, except for the egg whites. Add egg whites last. Pour small amount of batter onto a hot buttered cast-iron griddle. When pancakes begin to bubble, turn over and brown other side. Remove to plate. Spread pancakes with preserves, jam, or jelly and 1 tablespoon whipped cream. Fold into triangles. Serve with afternoon coffee or as special dessert. Makes 4 to 5 dozen small pancakes.

—*Embassy of Iceland, Washington, D.C.*

●●●●●●●●●●●●●●●●●●●●●●●●●●●

Icelandic Rhubarb Sauce

Illustration from: Åt Solsidan, *1910*

1 pound fresh rhubarb
5 cups water
Sugar to taste
1 tablespoon potato flour or cornstarch

Wash rhubarb stalks and cut into small pieces. Boil in water for about 5 minutes. Sweeten with sugar. Remove from heat and stir in potato flour or cornstarch that has already been dissolved in a little water. Mix well and serve as a dessert with hard biscuits.

—*Dua Clemensen, Independence, Missouri*

Lingonberry Dessert
Swedish

4 bread rusks, broken into small pieces
1 quart lingonberry sauce
1 14-ounce can pears, drained and cubed
Whipped cream

Mix ingredients together. Refrigerate for two hours. Serve in glass or crystal parfait glasses. Top with whipped cream.

Lingonberry Mousse
Swedish

1 1/3 cups heavy cream
2 tablespoons sugar
4 egg yolks
1 1/2 tablespoons gelatin, softened in 1/4 cup cold water

3 cups lingonberries in syrup, puréed
1 quart heavy cream, whipped to soft peaks
Fresh fruit and mint leaves (optional)

Bring the 1 1/3 cups cream and 2 tablespoons sugar to a boil. Pour into gently beaten egg yolks, whisking continuously. Return to stove and cook over low heat until mixture coats spoon. Mix in the softened gelatin and puréed lingonberries. Place pan of mixture over ice, stirring constantly, until mixture is cool and thick, but not set. Fold in whipped cream. Refrigerate until firm. Spoon into parfait dishes and garnish with fresh fruit and mint leaves. Serves 8 to 10.

Norwegian Almonds

3/4 cup large-size almonds
3/4 cup sugar

3/4 cup water
Red food coloring

Wash almonds in cold water. Place sugar, water, and a few drops of red food coloring in a large frying pan. Boil until water has evaporated and the sugar has melted. Add almonds and continue to cook until the sugar turns to caramel and adheres to the almonds. Stir frequently with wooden spoon. Pour caramelized almonds onto oiled cookie tin. While still warm, separate with two wooden spoons. Store in airtight container.

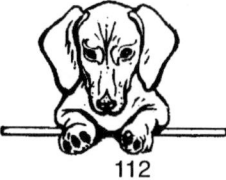

Illustration from: Andras Barn, *1913*

Norwegian Candied Orange Peel

6 oranges   Cold water
1 teaspoon salt

Peel oranges; remove membranes from the peels. Place peels in a saucepan; add salt and cover with cold water. Boil until tender, then drain and cut peels into strips.

Syrup:
1 1/2 cups water   1/4 cup honey
2 cups sugar

Place all ingredients for syrup in a pan; add the prepared orange peel and cook over low heat until peels absorb the syrup. Cool slightly until peels are sugar-coated and dry. Remove peels from pan and spread on waxed paper to cool thoroughly. Store in airtight container.

Pear-i-sian Delight
Swedish

4 to 5 fresh ripe pears
2 cups water

3/4 cup sugar

Wash pears. Cut in quarters, lengthwise. Remove cores. Place in shallow pan and add about 2 cups water. Sprinkle with sugar. Bring to a boil. Reduce heat and simmer for 5 minutes. Place cooked pears in individual serving dishes.

Almond topping:
1/4 cup butter
1/2 cup sugar
2 tablespoons flour
1/4 cup milk

1 teaspoon vanilla
2/3 cup sliced almonds
Whipped cream (optional)
Maraschino cherries or strawberries
(optional)

Melt butter in small saucepan; stir in sugar, flour, and milk. Stir and cook over low heat until mixture thickens. Stir in vanilla and almonds. Spoon over pears; serve immediately, or refrigerate until serving time. Garnish with spoonfuls of whipped cream and maraschino cherries or strawberries if desired. Serves 10.

Sarah Bernhardt Dessert

Danish

This dessert, a chocolate-topped macaroon base with chocolate truffle filling, was named for the French actress upon her visit to Copenhagen in 1880.

Macaroon base:
3 1/2 ounces almond paste
1 cup sugar
2 or 3 egg whites

Chocolate truffle filling:
4 ounces unsweetened chocolate
2 cups whipped cream

Macaroon base: Mix almond paste and sugar together. Add egg whites and blend to a porridge-like consistency. Divide mixture into approximately 10 parts and place on baking sheet. Bake 30 minutes at 350°.

Chocolate truffle filling: Melt chocolate. Blend half melted chocolate into whipped cream; chill, then spread chilled chocolate mixture on each macaroon base. Dip the top of the confection into the remaining chocolate. Refrigerate 2 to 3 hours.

—*Conditoriet La Glace, Copenhagen, Denmark*

Skyr
Icelandic Milk Curd

4 quarts plus 1/2 cup milk
2 tablespoons starter* (see below)

1/4 rennet tablet, dissolved in
1 tablespoon water

In large pan, scald 4 quarts milk. Let cool to lukewarm. Stir together the 1/2 cup milk and starter until smooth. Add the rennet tablet that has been dissolved in water. Mix into the lukewarm milk and stir well. Set aside in a warm place in a large crock or container. Cover with a heavy towel for about 24 hours. The milk should curdle. Strain whey from curd using a bag made of thin muslin or three thicknesses of cheesecloth. Stir well and serve with sugar and cream. Save 2 tablespoons of the Skyr to use as starter.

*Note: If you do not have Skyr to use for starter: combine 1 egg, 1/2 cup sour cream, and 1 tablespoon sugar. Mix thoroughly.

Swedish Candy
Knäck

1 cup white sugar
1 cup dark corn syrup
1/4 cup butter

1 cup half-and-half
1/3 cup almonds, chopped

Mix sugar, corn syrup, butter, and half-and-half in a heavy saucepan or skillet. Cook over low heat, stirring continuously, until mixture reaches 250° on a candy thermometer, or soft ball stage. This takes 30 to 45 minutes. Add almonds and pour into small foil candy cup forms. Allow to set. Store in airtight container.

Swedish Nuts

2 egg whites
1 cup sugar
4 cups pecans, walnuts, or almonds

1/2 cup butter or margarine
Pinch of salt

Beat egg whites until frothy. Add sugar a little at a time and continue to beat until stiff. Fold in nuts. Melt butter in a 13x9x2-inch cake pan. Add a pinch of salt. Spread meringue nut mixture over the butter and bake at 350° for about 30 minutes. Stir mixture about every 10 minutes with wooden spoon, spooning butter over the nuts. When done, the nuts will be coated with a caramel-like coating. Spread on waxed paper to cool. Store in airtight container.

BOOKS BY MAIL Stocking Stuffers Postpaid You may mix titles. One book for $12.95; two for $21.00; three for $29.00; four for $36.00; six for $52.00; twelve for $95.00. 2010 Prices subject to change.

Æbleskiver and More (Danish)
American Gothic Cookbook
Amish Mennonite Recipes
Buffets and Potlucks
Cherished Czech Recipes
Czech & Slovak Kolaches
   & Sweet Treats
Dandy Dutch Recipes
Dear Danish Recipes
Dutch Style Recipes
Fine Finnish Foods
Fire in the Bowl: Favorite Chili Recipes
French Recipes
German Style Recipes
Great German Recipes

Healthy Recipes
Microwave Recipes
Norwegian Centennial Recipes
Norwegian Recipes
Pleasing Polish Recipes
Quality Czech Mushroom Recipes
Quality Dumpling Recipes
Recipes from Ireland
Recipes from Old Mexico
Savory Scottish Recipes
Scandinavian Holiday Recipes
Scandinavian Smorgasbord Recipes
Scandinavian Sweet Treats
Scandinavian Style Fish and Seafood
Slavic Specialties

Slovak Recipes
Splendid Swedish Recipes
Tales from Texas Tables
Texas Cookoff
Time-Honored Norwegian Recipes
Ukrainian Recipes
Waffles, Flapjacks, Pancakes from
   Scandinavia and Around the World

License to Cook Series:
Alaska Style; Arizona Style;
Iowa Style; Italian Style;
Minnesota Style; Missouri Style;
New Mexico Style;
Oregon Style; Texas Style;
and Wisconsin Style

PENFIELD BOOKS, 215 BROWN STREET, IOWA CITY, IA 52245-5801 • 1-800-728-9998 • www.penfieldbooks.com

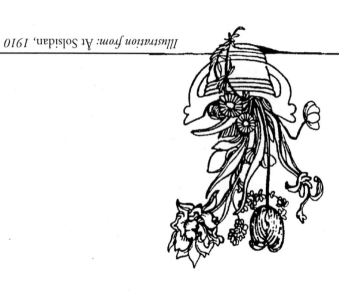